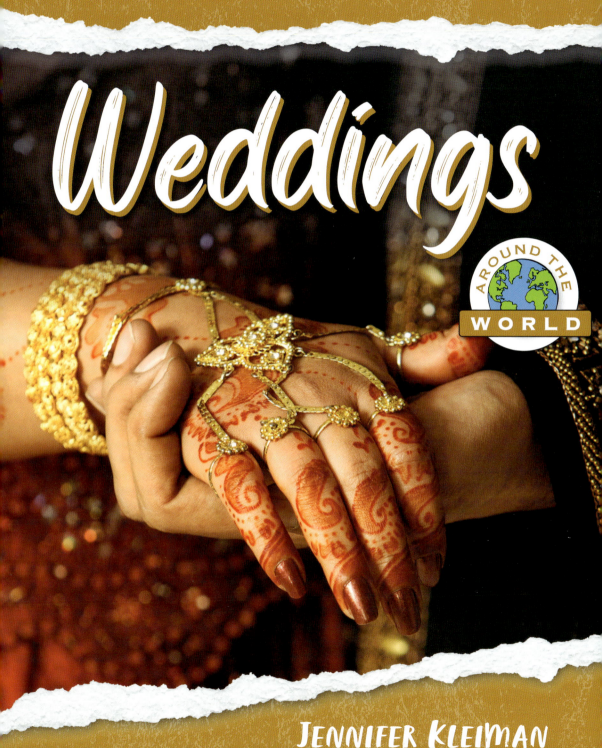

How the World Celebrates

Weddings

Around the World

Jennifer Kleiman

45TH PARALLEL PRESS

Published in the United States of America by Cherry Lake Publishing Group
Ann Arbor, Michigan
www.cherrylakepublishing.com

Reading Adviser: Beth Walker Gambro, MS, Ed., Reading Consultant, Yorkville, IL

Photo Credits: © Omer N Raja/Shutterstock, cover, title page; © pixelheadphoto digitalskillet/Shutterstock, 4; © Françoise Foliot via Wikimedia Commons CC BY-SA 4.0, 6; © Vietnam Colors/Shutterstock, 7; © pixelheadphoto digitalskillet/Shutterstock, 8; © pixelheadphoto digitalskillet/Shutterstock, 10; © pixelheadphoto digitalskillet/Shutterstock, 13; © Abm-25/Shutterstock, 14; © Zeeshan Tejani/Alamy Stock Photo, 16; © IVASHstudio/Shutterstock, 18; © LiliGraphie/Shutterstock, 20; © Dennis Diatel/Shutterstock, 23; © Valera.raw/Shutterstock, 24; © Dima Shetinin/Shutterstock, 27; © Evgeniy pavlovski/Shutterstock, 28; © Pyty/Shutterstock, 30

Copyright © 2025 by Cherry Lake Publishing Group
All rights reserved. No part of this book may be reproduced or utilized in any form or by any means without written permission from the publisher.

45th Parallel Press is an imprint of Cherry Lake Publishing Group.

Library of Congress Cataloging-in-Publication Data

Names: Kleiman, Jennifer, 1978- author.
Title: Weddings around the world / written by Jennifer Kleiman.
Description: Ann Arbor, MI : 45th Parallel Press, 2025. | Series: How the world celebrates | Audience: Grades 4-6 | Summary: "Weddings bring families, friends, and communities together to celebrate love and the start of something new. Readers will explore wedding customs and traditions around the world. This hi-lo narrative nonfiction series celebrates diverse cultures while highlighting how expressions of joy and connection are all part of the human experience"-- Provided by publisher.
Identifiers: LCCN 2024036517 | ISBN 9781668956571 (hardcover) | ISBN 9781668957424 (paperback) | ISBN 9781668958292 (ebook) | ISBN 9781668959169 (pdf)
Subjects: LCSH: Marriage customs and rites--Juvenile literature. | Weddings--Juvenile literature.
Classification: LCC GT2690 .K54 2025 | DDC 369.5--dc23/eng/20240918
LC record available at https://lccn.loc.gov/2024036517

Cherry Lake Publishing would like to acknowledge the work of the Partnership for 21st Century Learning, a network of Battelle for Kids. Please visit Battelle for Kids online for more information.

Printed in the United States of America

NOTE FROM PUBLISHER: Websites change regularly, and their future contents are outside of our control. Supervise children when conducting any recommended online searches for extended learning opportunities.

Table of Contents

INTRODUCTION	5
CHAPTER 1: An American Wedding	9
CHAPTER 2: A Pakistani Wedding	15
CHAPTER 3: A German Wedding	19
CHAPTER 4: An Israeli Wedding	25
FAST FACTS: Map of Unusual Wedding Traditions	30
LEARN MORE	31
GLOSSARY	32
INDEX	32
ABOUT THE AUTHOR	32

DID YOU KNOW? Wedding rings are worn on the left hand. This is because of a vein in the fourth finger. It was once believed to lead directly to the heart.

Introduction

Birth. Puberty. Marriage. Death. Throughout history, these events have had sacred importance. They mark major transitions in life. We celebrate them through ceremonies.

A wedding is a marriage ceremony. It celebrates the union of 2 people. Weddings are times of joy. Almost every culture has them. Yet they can all look quite different. Some weddings are religious. They incorporate specific rituals, blessings, and prayers. They are performed by religious leaders. The union is recognized by God or other religious beings.

Others choose a civil ceremony. A civil marriage can be performed by a government official. It can also be performed by any **officiant**. An officiant has a license to marry people. The union is recognized by law.

Most weddings include a bit of both. A couple might choose a religious ceremony. However, they must still obtain a wedding license. This makes the marriage legally recognized.

DID YOU KNOW?
Weddings can also vary by race, class, religion, and sexual orientation. They can look different around the world. Different cultures have their own traditions and customs. They are unique to people's way of life.

THE HISTORY OF MARRIAGE

Marriage dates back at least 4,350 years. The first marriage on record was in 2350 BCE. It took place in Mesopotamia. That's modern-day Iraq.

Ancient marriage had little to do with love. It was a practical arrangement. It was mostly for producing children. It joined certain families together. It ensured the survival of those clans. Ancient wedding rituals reflect this. The couple promised to take care of each other. They promised to take care of their children.

People did not often get to choose who they married. Their families chose. Sometimes the king or ruler chose. Men often had more choice. In some places, women were treated like property. Fathers made choices for them. Then husbands did.

THE EVOLUTION OF MARRIAGE

Over time, religion played a bigger role. Weddings became ceremonies asking for God's grace. **Vows** included promises to God. A vow is a solemn promise.

Marrying for love was not common until the 18th century. In Western culture, people began focusing on personal happiness. People picked their own partners. Love became the most important factor in their choice. Eastern cultures are different. Practical considerations may still outrank love. Couples build a life together. They grow together. Their bond keeps families strong.

Chapter 1
An American Wedding

Today, Mia and Marcus are getting married. Mia is Sasha's sister. Sasha watches Mia get ready. Mia's white gown trails to the floor. It gathers behind her in a sequined pool. Sasha's mother fastens a necklace around Mia's neck. A large blue stone hangs from the center.

"I want you to wear this today," she says. "It belonged to my grandmother. I added a new chain."

"Something old, something new, something borrowed, something blue," Sasha recites. It is an old wedding saying. Following it is believed to bring good luck.

Sasha tugs at her own dress. In many weddings, bridesmaids dress the same. They stand beside the bride at the wedding. Sasha is Mia's maid of honor. She will stand closest to Mia.

The church is filled with guests. The bride's guests sit on one side. The groom's guests sit on the other. Everyone wears formal clothes.

Once the music begins, it is time for the **processional**. That is when people walk down the aisle in a specific order. Sasha waits her turn. She is nervous but excited.

The groom's parents are first. They take a seat in the front row. Next comes Sasha's mother. She is followed by the pastor. He is the wedding officiant. He takes his place at the altar.

Then comes the groom and his best man in their tuxedos. Marcus chose his sister, Dana, as his best man. It is an **unconventional**, or uncommon, choice. Marcus is a great brother.

Sasha is happy he will be her brother-in-law. The bridesmaids and groomsmen follow in pairs.

After that, it's Sasha's turn. The maid of honor must walk alone. She takes a deep breath. She steps carefully. She hopes she does not trip.

Sasha's little brother is the ring bearer. He carries the wedding rings on a velvet pillow. He hands them to Dana. She will hold onto them until the couple exchanges rings. The flower girl follows. She sprinkles flower petals for Mia to walk on.

The music stops. The organ player begins "Here Comes the Bride." It's a traditional song to introduce the bride. Sasha's father escorts Mia down the aisle. All of the guests turn to watch. Cameras flash like dozens of fireflies. Sasha can't help but smile. Mia looks so beautiful. And she looks so happy. Mia smiles at Marcus. She takes his hand.

The pastor welcomes everyone. He says a few words about Mia and Marcus. Then the couple exchanges wedding vows. Mia and Marcus vow to love, honor, and respect one another. They vow to take care of each other in sickness and health. They exchange rings.

The pastor introduces the couple as husband and wife. He invites them to share a kiss. It is a symbol of their union. The crowd applauds. Marcus is now part of the family!

The wedding reception is at a hotel. The ballroom is filled with dinner tables. They are covered in white tablecloths. Name cards tell the guests where to sit. Sasha sits at the table with her family. The newlyweds sit at a table in front of the room.

Someone taps their glass with a fork. Others follow. It is a fun tradition at wedding receptions. It means the couple should kiss.

After the main course, Sasha's father gives a toast. He welcomes Marcus to the family. Several other people give toasts. They talk about the couple's love for each other. They share stories about them.

Dinner is followed by dancing. It begins with the couple's first dance. Sasha's father then dances with Mia. Her mother dances with Marcus. Soon everyone is dancing.

It is time to cut the cake. Mia and Marcus both hold the knife. They cut the cake together. They feed it to each other. This symbolizes their first task as a married couple.

All that's left is the bouquet toss. All the unmarried people gather. Mia turns her back to the crowd. She tosses her bouquet over her head. One of the bridesmaids catches it. This predicts she will be the next to marry.

DID YOU KNOW? People used to throw rice at weddings. It symbolizes **fertility**, or the ability to produce. Many wedding venues have banned rice. It is hard to clean up and a safety hazard. They also fear it could harm birds.

Outside, the guests wait for the couple. They are getting changed. Mia and Marcus will leave together. It symbolizes their new start in life. The couple's car is parked in front. Mia and Marcus's friends have decorated it. Sasha and Dana helped.

The couple exits to a shower of birdseed. Everyone tosses a handful at the newlyweds. Sasha hugs her sister goodbye. She wishes her well.

PAKISTANI WEDDINGS are elaborate affairs. They last 3 to 7 days. They include celebrations before and after the wedding ceremony. Modern couples choose which traditions and ceremonies to include. They may adapt or combine some of them.

Chapter 2
A Pakistani Wedding

In 1 week, Inaya will marry Hamza. First comes the *Dholki* ceremony. Inaya sits with the *dohl* between her legs. She beats the double-headed drum. The rhythm is steady and unbroken. Her sister Faiza sits across from her. She taps a silver spoon on the drum. Auntie plays the tambourine.

Family members make a circle around the women. So do members of the wedding party. Everyone listens. They sing along. They dance. Inaya taught Faiza dance steps when they were younger. They laugh and dance together again. Once they are tired, they eat.

Next comes the *Mayoun*. Women gather at Faiza's home. Inaya kneels in a yellow dress. She does not wear makeup. Their mother sits beside her. Faiza puts flower rings on Inaya. She adds flower earrings. Inaya's friends rub a lotion containing the spice turmeric on her skin. It will help her skin glow. Faiza thinks she glows anyway.

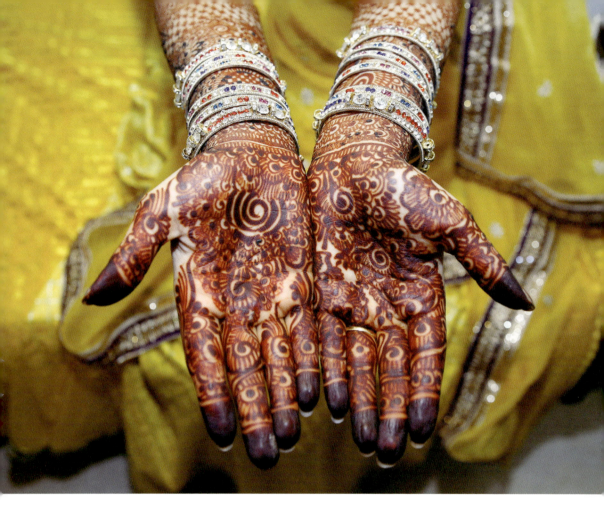

Two days later comes the *Mehndi* ceremony. It is the day before the wedding. Inaya and Hamza sit together. Inaya presents her palms to the Mehndi artist. The artist makes elaborate Arabic designs in golden **henna**, a reddish-brown dye. Seven happily married women feed the bride and groom fruit. Meanwhile, everyone dances to **Bollywood** music. Bollywood is the Indian movie industry. Afterward, they feast.

The *Nikah* is the most important part of the wedding. It is the Islamic marriage contract ceremony. The couples and their families arrive at the **mosque**. It is a place of Islamic worship. Everyone removes their shoes out of respect. They recite religious verses.

Faiza and other girls and women stay in one area. Men stay in the other. Inaya and Hamza exchange vows. They sign the marriage contract in front of the **imam**. An imam is an Islamic religious leader.

The *Walima* is held the next day. This is the wedding banquet. Hamza's family hosts. Friends and family are invited to attend. The men wear suits. The women are draped in saris. People feast and dance. They take pictures of the couple. They present gifts.

The *Baraat* follows. It is the groom's procession. The procession begins at Hamza's home. It ends at Inaya's. Hamza arrives on a beautiful white horse. The horse is decorated to match Hamza's clothing. Everything is festive and magical. Faiza feels like she has been smiling for days! There is music, dancing, and fireworks. When it ends, it is time for Faiza to bid her sister farewell. She holds her extra tight. Their father holds the Qur'an over Inaya's head. That is the Islamic holy book. He gives them a blessing. Inaya and Hamza leave together. They begin their life as one.

In **GERMANY**, all couples are legally required to have a civil wedding ceremony. It takes place at a registry office. Couples can choose to have a religious ceremony afterward. Today, only about 1 in 5 couples do.

Chapter 3
A German Wedding

Tomorrow, Adele and Claus will marry. Tonight is their *Polterabend*. Claus is Johann's cousin. Johann and his parents carry plates. They go to Adele's house. Ahead of them is Herr Müller. He carries an old toilet bowl. He sets it down in the yard with a grunt.

"*Guten abend*!" he greets Adele's father, Karl. "Good evening!"

"A toilet bowl!" Karl remarks.

Herr Müller winks. "I can't wait to smash it in your driveway!"

All the guests bring something to smash. That is why Johann has a stack of plates. It is good luck for the couple. Guests bring old cups, bowls, and vases. Claus's brother brings a sink. Mirrors are *verboten*, or forbidden. So is glass. Breaking them is bad luck.

Everyone makes a terrible mess of the front yard. It is loud and unruly. It's supposed to be. Polterabend means an "evening of making a racket." It will be Adele and Claus's job to clean it up. It will show their teamwork. Johann laughs with his cousins as they smash each plate.

Adele and Claus submitted an application to marry. It took many months for approval. Then they had to secure an appointment at the registry. The long wait has finally ended. They are allowed to marry.

The ceremony takes place in one of the wedding rooms at city hall. It is conducted by a justice of the peace. Guests are not typically invited. Johann's mother tells him about it. Adele and Claus will walk down the aisle together. They will walk as close as possible. This keeps anything from coming between them. Adele chose a white dress and a veil. She will have a penny in her shoe for luck. Claus chose a dark suit.

It is evening. Guests gather outside before the wedding reception. They wait for the couple to arrive. Adele and Claus's first married task is the *Baumstamm sägen*. This is the log-cutting ceremony. They must work together to saw a log in half. It shows that the couple can achieve anything together.

Adele and Claus stand on either side of the log. They are still wearing their wedding clothes. They move the saw's blade back and forth. Everyone cheers them on. Johann cheers as loud as he can. Guests toss rice at the couple. A few grains land in Adele's hair. The number of grains represents the number of children they will have.

The wedding reception is filled with food, fun, and dancing. The couple's dance comes first. Adele and Claus dance the waltz. This is the ceremonial first dance as a couple. Johann will learn to waltz in high school. He hopes he will dance as well as Claus does.

After dinner, the couple's fathers give toasts. Adele and Claus share a drink from the bridal cup. This 2-sided cup is shaped like a **maiden**. A maiden is an unmarried woman. The maiden holds one cup over her head. It is on a hinge so it can swivel.

DID YOU KNOW?

Traditionally, German brides wore black wedding dresses and white veils. They also saved pennies to buy wedding shoes. German brides would save their pennies for years. They bought their shoes with them. This started the marriage off on the right foot.

The maiden's skirt is also a cup. The couple drinks from each end at the same time. They make a game of it. The game is called "Who Rules the Nest?" The first to finish rules the nest! Everyone cheers as Adele wins.

Another fun part of the evening is the *spitzwecken*. This is the cake ceremony. The cake is 10 feet (3 meters) tall. It sits on a long wooden board. A group of guests try to carry it through the door. They grunt and groan. They pause for a drink. Everyone laughs. This is all part of the fun.

"It won't fit," says Carl. He is Claus's best man. "We'll have to cut it in half!" Everyone cheers as they cut it.

The reception lasts long into the evening. At midnight, it is time for the veil dance. The unmarried women hold up Adele's veil. They make a canopy of it. Adele and Claus dance beneath it. While they dance, the women tear the veil to shreds. Cousin Ella ends up with the largest piece. This predicts she will be the next to marry.

It is late. It is time for Adele and Claus to leave. The guests have blocked the door with ribbons. The couple must pay a toll to exit. For payment, the couple vows to throw another party.

"*Wir versprechen,*" Adele and Claus laugh. "We promise." Johann helps Carl pull down the ribbons. Adele and Claus bid their guests farewell. Johann can't wait for the next party.

Most **ISRAELI WEDDINGS** are Jewish. About 74 percent of Israelis are Jewish. Religious and non-religious Jews have different customs. So do Jews from different parts of the world. Wedding ceremonies reflect this. Israel is filled with immigrants. They come from North Africa and the Middle East. They also come from Europe and North America. Because of this, some weddings also incorporate traditions from other countries.

Chapter 4
An Israeli Wedding

Shira and Levi are to be wed. Adam is Levi's brother. He's never seen Levi this happy. It is the Shabbat, or Sabbath, before the wedding. The rabbi invites the couple to read from the **Torah**. The Torah is the first 5 books of the Hebrew Bible. The ritual is called an *aufruf*. After their reading, the rabbi blesses the couple. Then all the congregants make a circle around them. Adam sings and dances with them. He throws candy at the happy couple. Many others do too. It symbolizes the sweetness of marriage. "*Mazel tov*!" they all shout. "Congratulations!"

Shira and Levi don't see each other for several days. This tradition is said to increase their love for each other. Levi stays at his parents' house. He says his apartment is too lonely. He tells Adam that Shira is at her *Mikvah* immersion. This is a ritual bath. Brides do this the night before the wedding. The Mikvah is a pool of natural water. It marks the passage from being single to married.

The wedding begins with a reception. There are 2 separate rooms. One is for Shira. The other is for Levi. Drinks and appetizers are served. Guests flow freely from one room to the other. Adam stays close to his father. They visit with family members and friends.

Before the ceremony, Shira and Levi sign the *Ketubah.* It is a Jewish wedding contract. It outlines the couple's responsibilities to each other. It is also a beautiful piece of art. The couple will frame it. They will hang it in their home. Adam's aunt is a Ketubah artist. One of her first ones was for Adam's mom and dad's wedding. It still hangs in their house.

Signing the Ketubah is a sacred ritual. Each has chosen a friend to witness the signing. The witnesses cannot be blood relatives.

DID YOU KNOW?

Traditionally, the aufruf is only for the groom. Modern weddings often include the bride too. Other Jewish cultures call it the *shabbat chatan.* It takes place after the wedding.

The ceremony begins with the *Bedeken*. Adam dances Levi into the room with other friends and family. Shira is seated. Her mother and mother-in-law sit next to her. Levi gently lifts Shira's wedding veil. He covers her face with it. This symbolizes his love for her inner beauty. He recites a blessing.

Shira's and Levi's parents walk them to the *chuppah*. This is the wedding canopy. It represents the groom's home. The rabbi is waiting for them.

Shira begins by circling Levi 7 times. Seven is a sacred number in Judaism. Then the rabbi recites marriage blessings over wine. The couple drinks. Afterward, Levi slips a plain gold band on Shira's finger. The groom must give the bride something of value. By Jewish law, this makes the marriage official.

The rabbi reads the Ketubah out loud. He hands it to Levi. Levi gives the document to Shira. It becomes the bride's property.

Shira and Levi invite friends and family to the chuppah. They each take turns reading the 7 blessings. Then a second cup of wine is shared.

The ceremony ends with the breaking of the glass. The rabbi covers the glass in white linen. He places it on the floor. Levi brings his foot down hard.

> **DID YOU KNOW?** A Jewish wedding is followed by 7 days of celebration. It is called 7 Days of Feasting. During those days, the couple does not work. They only eat, drink, and rejoice. Friends and family members host festive meals.

"Mazel tov!" everyone shouts. After the ceremony, Shira and Levi spend a few moments alone. This is called the *Yichud*. The couple has not spent time alone in several days. The Yichud is a moment of private reflection. The couple reflects on what has taken place.

At last, it is officially time to celebrate! Shira and Levi rejoin their guests. It is time for dinner and dancing.

The wedding feast is called the *seudat* **mitzvah**. It is a sacred meal. A mitzvah is a commandment from God. The evening is filled with joyful dancing. It is a mitzvah to bring joy to the couple. "Hava Nagila" plays. It is a Jewish folk song. It is time to dance the hora. Shira and Levi are seated in chairs. The guests form a circle around them. The music starts slowly. Then it picks up speed. The guests dance faster and faster. They lift the chairs into the air. Shira and Levi each hold one end of a cloth napkin. It is a symbol of their union. Adam sings and dances. He laughs and cheers.

FAST FACTS: MAP OF UNUSUAL WEDDING TRADITIONS

① **SCOTLAND:** Friends and family cover the couple in messy substances, like eggs and mud.

② **TURKEY:** The bride makes her groom a coffee. She flavors it with salt instead of sugar.

③ **TUJIA, CHINA:** Brides cry for an hour every day for a month. Other women in their family join in.

④ **INDIA:** The bride's family steals the groom's shoes. The groom must pay to get them back.

⑤ **KENYA:** The father of the bride spits on the bride for good luck.

⑥ **NIGERIA:** Guests throw cash at the newly married couple.

⑦ **VENEZUELA:** The newlyweds sneak out of the reception.

⑧ **CUBA:** Guests pay to dance with the bride.

⑨ **AUSTRALIA:** Guests hold stones during the ceremony.

⑩ **MALAYSIA:** The bride and groom cannot use the bathroom for 3 days after the wedding.

LEARN MORE

BOOKS:
Bradley, Fleur. *My Life as a Muslim.* Ann Arbor, MI: 45th Parallel Press, 2022.

Kaminski, Leah. *Assalam-o-Alaikum,* Pakistan. Ann Arbor, MI: Cherry Lake Publishing, 2020.

Kleiman, Jennifer. *My Life as a Jew.* Ann Arbor, MI: 45th Parallel Press, 2024.

ONLINE:
With an adult, explore more online with these suggested searches.

- "Marriage," Kids Britannica
- "What Is Mehndi?" Twinkl

GLOSSARY

Bollywood (BAH-lee-wuhd) the movie industry in India

fertility (fuhr-TIH-luh-tee) capable of producing, as in crops or offspring

henna (HEH-nuh) a reddish-brown dye used to paint temporary tattoos

imam (ih-MAHM) the person who leads prayers in a mosque

maiden (MAY-duhn) an unmarried girl or woman

mitzvah (MITS-vuh) a commandment of the Jewish law

mosque (MAHSK) a building used for worship by Muslims

officiant (uh-FIH-shee-uhnt) someone who officially performs a ceremony such as a wedding

processional (pruh-SEH-shuh-nahl) a group of individuals moving in a ceremonial way

Torah (TOR-uh) the first 5 books of the Hebrew Bible

unconventional (uhn-kuhn-VEN-shuh-nuhl) out of the ordinary

vow (VOW) a solemn promise

INDEX

American weddings, 9–13
aufruf, 25, 26

Baraat, 17

Christian marriage rites, 11
civil ceremonies, 5, 6, 18, 21

dancing and music, 11, 12, 15, 17, 22–23, 27, 29
Dholki ceremony, 15
dress and grooming, 7, 8–9, 14, 15–16, 20, 21, 22–23, 27

German weddings, 18–23

history of marriage, 6–7

Islamic marriage rites, 16–17
Israeli weddings, 24–29

Jewish marriage rites, 25–28

Ketubah, 26, 28

love, 6, 7, 11, 12, 25, 27

marriage, 5–11
Mayoun, 15
Mehndi ceremony, 16
music and dancing, 11, 12, 15, 17, 22–23, 27, 29
Muslim marriage rites, 16–17

Nikah, 16

officiants, 5, 10, 11, 17, 21, 27–28

Pakistani weddings, 14–17
Polterabend, 19

religious ceremonies, 5, 7, 16–17, 18, 24, 25–29
rings, 4, 11, 27

symbolism, 4, 11, 12, 13, 25, 27, 28, 29

traditions, 6–7, 9, 11–13, 14, 15, 19–20, 21–23, 24, 25–29, 30

vows, 7, 11, 17

Walima, 17

ABOUT THE AUTHOR

Jennifer Kleiman has worked in educational publishing for more than 20 years. Today, she is a busy writer and editor, working on her second novel. She lives in Chicago, in a rickety old house, with her wife, 2 cats, a dog named Helen, and a yard full of chickens.